The Greatest Gift of All

REFLECTIONS AND PRAYERS FOR THE CHRISTMAS SEASON

Mark G. Boyer

Dedicated to Karl and Sheri Kinler
and their children: Amy, Dory and Zachary

The Greatest Gift of All
Reflections and Prayers for the Christmas Season
by Mark G. Boyer

Edited by Kass Dotterweich
Cover Design by John Macia
Typesetting by Garrison Publications

All biblical quotations are taken from the *Contemporary English Version*, copyright © 1995, American Bible Society, 1865 Broadway, New York, NY 10023. Used with permission. All rights reserved.

Copyright © 1999 by Mark G. Boyer

Published by   ACTA Publications
              Assisting Christians To Act
              4848 N. Clark Street
              Chicago, IL 60640
              800-397-2282

All rights reserved. No part of this publication may be reproduced or transmitted in any form or by any means, electronic or mechanical, including photocopying and recording, or by any information storage and retrieval system, without permission from the publisher.

Library of Congress Catalog number: 99-65632

ISBN: 0-87946-206-X

Printed in the United States of America

99 00 01 02 03 year/printing 5 4 3 2 1 First Printing

Contents

Introduction 5
Advent 8
Angels 10
Baptism 12
Bells 14
Candles 16
Cards 18
Cookies 20
Dove 22
Dromedary 24
Evergreen 26
Family 28
Frankincense 30
Gloria 32
Gold 34
Holly 36
Innocents 38
Jesus 40
Joachim and Anne 42
Joseph 44
Kings 46
Lucy 48
Manger 50
Mary 52

Myrrh	54
Nativity	56
Nicholas	58
Ornaments	60
Poinsettia	62
Quirinius	64
Ray	66
Redeemer	68
Reindeer	70
Shepherds and Sheep	72
Snow	74
Tree	76
Urn	78
Valley	80
Winter Solstice	82
Wreath	84
Xmas	86
Yule	88
Zenith	90
Blessings for Advent and Christmastime	92

Introduction

The Greatest Gift of All is designed to guide you into daily prayer experiences using the favorite people and things that surround you during the Christmas season. Perhaps it will become one of the Christmas treasures that you put away with the boxes of Advent and Christmas decorations every year, only to discover and use again a year later. Over the years, *The Greatest Gift of All* can become an heirloom that is passed to future generations, like so many of the special things of Christmastime.

This book follows the alphabet, from A to Z, and each reflection focuses on an aspect of the Christmas season. A book arranged alphabetically is called an "abecedarian," a word that also describes one who is learning the basics of an idea or theme—in this case, the holiness of the home and the people who live in it at Christmastime.

This book offers forty-two entries, each consisting of six parts: Title, Scripture, Reflection, Meditation, Prayer and Memories. The Title is a person or thing in the home. The Scripture is taken from either the Hebrew Bible (Old Testament) or the Christian Bible (New Testament) and establishes the topic's everyday people and things in our faith tradition. The Reflection stimulates your thoughts and helps you make a connection between God and the celebration of Christmas. The Meditation encourages personal contemplation or journaling to chronicle your spiritual growth. The Prayer, a few verses from a psalm, summarizes the ideas presented in the Scripture, the Reflection, and the Meditation. (In order to make the Prayer flow, I have not marked ellipses where text has been deleted.)

The section titled Memories contains suggestions for your own personal record-keeping. I used to have a great aunt who decorated her home with a huge Christmas tree every year and filled its branches with hundreds of ornaments. Each ornament had a story that went with it. When my aunt died, however, the stories died with her, because no one ever recorded them. The Memories section gives you ideas for recording your stories about the people and things of Christmas in your home. As you record these memories, perhaps in a special bound blank book just for that purpose, keep in mind that you are recording some of your family's most precious history.

Beginning on page 92 you will find "Blessings for Advent and Christmastime." These short family prayers bless all that is part of your home during this season. They can be used and adapted as you see fit.

It is my hope that, through the use of this book, you will be awakened to God's presence through the people and things of the Christmas season—this year and for many years to come.

When the time was right,
God sent his Son,
and a woman gave birth to him.
Galatians 4:4

Advent

Scripture

I pray that you will be blessed with kindness and peace from God, who is and was and is coming (Revelation 1:4).

Reflection

The word "Advent" is formed by the merger of two Latin words: the prefix *ad*, meaning "to" or "toward," and the verb *venire*, meaning "to come." Thus "Advent" means "to come toward."

We can look at the season of Advent, the four weeks before Christmas, in two ways. We can enter into this season as a journey toward Christmas, counting down the weeks and days with wonder and anticipation. Or we can enter these weeks with a quiet stillness, letting Christmas travel toward us.

There is a third approach to Advent: Christ is coming. While Christmas Day is expected, the coming of Christ seldom is; Christ comes as a surprise. He enters our homes in those who live with us through their prayer, anticipation and cooperation. He is brought into our homes by relatives who bear gifts of food and clothes and items for our homes. He comes toward us in any type of kindness another bestows upon us—and we bear Christ to others by doing the same. This is the unexpected dimension of Advent: the coming of Christ through others. This is what makes Advent a season of surprise and joy. With this understanding, we can see that Christmas is not just a once-a-year celebration; it happens every day.

Meditation

Who comes to visit you during Advent and the Christmas holidays? How is each visitor an incarnation of Christ? Whom do you visit during Advent and the Christmas holidays? How do you bring Christ to them?

Prayer

Tell the heavens and the earth to be glad and celebrate! Command the ocean to roar with all its creatures and the fields to rejoice with all their crops. Then every tree in the forest will sing joyful songs to the Lord. He is coming to judge all people on earth with fairness and truth (Psalm 96:11-13).

Memories

Make a list of the names of people who visit you during the holidays, and note how each brings Christ into your home. Be sure to record the date each guest visits. Make this list each year.

Angels

Scripture

Suddenly many other angels came down from heaven and joined in praising God. They said: "Praise God in heaven! Peace on earth to everyone who pleases God" (Luke 2:13-14).

Reflection

When we hear the word "angel," most of us think of human beings with wings. Such creatures, however, do not exist. "Angel" was originally a verb—"to angel"—and was a biblical attempt to describe a manifestation, a flashing, a revelation of God's presence. Thus "angel" is but one of the myriad possibilities of who God is for us.

So awesome is God that God praises God's very self and moves us to do the same. God sends divine life, "angeling," to move all of us to sing God's praises. In the presence of the Spirit-conceived child, Jesus, God can do nothing less than offer praise upon his birth.

God reveals to shepherds in the fields that Jesus' birth has taken place, that God's name, Emanuel—meaning "God-with-us"—is an incarnate reality. At first the shepherds are afraid, as anyone should be when God "angels," when God reveals transcendence to the world. But God calms all fear and fills those who receive divine life with peace, which in turn moves them to praise God, who "lives" in heaven but has chosen to be revealed on earth.

Meditation

What types of angel figurines do you display in your home? How do they remind you of God's revealing presence? How do they remind you that "angel" is a verb?

Prayer

All of you mighty angels, who obey God's commands, come and praise your Lord! All of you thousands who serve and obey God, come and praise your Lord! All of God's creation and all that he rules, come and praise your Lord! With all my heart I praise the Lord! (Psalm 103:20-23).

Memories

Make a list of the names of people who send you Christmas cards with angels on them. For each person, identify how he or she "angels" or manifests God's presence to you. If you have received an angel figurine as a gift, record the name of the giver and how he or she "angeled" or revealed God to you. Add to this list each year.

Baptism

Scripture

About that time Jesus came from Nazareth in Galilee, and John baptized him in the Jordan River. As soon as Jesus came out of the water, he saw the sky open and the Holy Spirit coming down to him like a dove (Mark 1:9-10).

Reflection

The Christmas season ends with the Feast of the Baptism of the Lord in the Jordan River. This feast is meant to be a parallel with the Easter Vigil, when we baptize the new members of the Church and renew our own baptismal promises. The Baptism of the Lord marks the transition between Christmas and Ordinary Time. We pass through one in order to get to the other.

Any type of crossing over or through water indicates a change in life, followed by a period of testing and then fullness of life. We see this three-fold pattern in the Israelites' crossing of the Sea of Reeds. They leave their old lifestyle of slavery behind in Egypt, cross into a new land, test God's faithfulness by demanding food and water and, finally, emerge fully alive.

The same pattern can be found in the story of Joshua leading the Israelites across the Jordan River into the promised land, the multiple crossings of the Jordan by the prophets Elijah and Elisha, and the story of Naaman the Syrian, who leaves his old beliefs behind, tests the word of the prophet Elisha, plunges himself into the Jordan, is cured of his leprosy, and declares God to be the only deity. Jesus, too, comes to the water, passes through it, is tested, and emerges fully alive.

Our baptism was also a crossing—one we need to renew over and over again. We discover the fullness of life as we repeatedly leave our old lives behind. Sure, we test God and others to see if the new ways are really better. Then, once the river is crossed, we settle down to enjoy our new way of living. Sooner or later, of course, another river appears on the horizon of our life's journey, and we go through the process again. But the Spirit always leads the way.

Meditation

What major "rivers" have you crossed during your lifetime journey (such as college, marriage, children, etc.)?

Prayer

When the sea looked at God, it ran away, and the Jordan River flowed upstream. Ask the sea why it ran away or ask the Jordan why it flowed upstream. Earth, you will tremble when the Lord God of Jacob comes near, because he turns solid rock into flowing streams and pools of water (Psalm 114:3, 5, 7-8).

Memories

Record the names of the members of your family and the date of each person's baptism. On the Feast of the Baptism of the Lord invite each person to dip his or her hand into a small bowl of water and share a story of crossing a "river" during the past year. Practice this tradition from year to year.

Bells

Scripture

At that time the words "Dedicated to the Lord" will be engraved on the bells worn by horses. In fact, every ordinary cooking pot in Jerusalem will be just as sacred to the Lord All-Powerful as the bowls used at the altar (Zechariah 14:20-21).

Reflection

Bells herald Christmas. "Sleigh bells ring; are you listening?" the song asks. Carillons pipe out the "Carol of the Bells" from bell towers, while bell choirs accompany carolers. We hear the tinkling of bells as we open doors—even as we view them on the cards we receive in the mail.

The prophet Zechariah unites the profane and the sacred—the world in which we live and the world in which God lives—and declares that all is holy. Even the most profane item, like a cooking pot, is sacred to God, says the prophet.

Just as the bells attached to the horses' bridles heralded the arrival of the animals and served as a warning to walkers to get out of the way—much like horns on cars and trucks do today—so do the bells of Christmas awaken us to God in our midst. Indeed, all good cheer of the season comes from the God who declares that everything and everyone is dedicated to the Lord.

Meditation

How have bells awakened you to the presence of God?

Prayer

Praise God with trumpets and all kinds of harps. Praise him with tambourines and dancing, with stringed instruments and woodwinds. Praise God with cymbals, with clashing cymbals. Let every living creature praise the Lord. (Psalm 150:3-6)

Memories

Make a list of the kinds of bells you display in your home at Christmastime. Identify where each bell came from, such as a gift, a purchase, an inheritance, etc. Add to this list each year as needed.

Candles

Scripture

The Scriptures say, "God commanded light to shine in the dark." Now God is shining in our hearts to let you know that his glory is seen in Jesus Christ (2 Corinthians 4:6).

Reflection

Most of us are familiar with Elton John's song, "Candle in the Wind," either the original version or the one he rewrote for the 1997 funeral of Diana, Princess of Wales. In his song, John compares death to a candle in the wind. After a length of years, the wind extinguishes the light.

Candles, each made of wax and a piece of string, decorate our homes during Advent and Christmas. Four purple or white candles may be found in our Advent wreath. Red and green ones may highlight the mantle of the fireplace or serve as a centerpiece for our dining room table.

While we no longer burn candles for our routine lighting needs, candlelight certainly sets a mood, an atmosphere, an ambiance for prayer, and the opportunity to reflect on the shortness of our lives. When our lives burn with the wax of God's grace, we emit the light of God's glory and bathe the world in the radiance of Jesus Christ, who is God's candle. The brilliant flame of that candle was relit after the cross blew it out, and continues to burn today, guiding us to eternal light and life.

Meditation

How is your life like a candle? How much of your candle is burned? How much remains? Where will you take your light today?

Prayer

Your love is faithful, Lord. You give your guests a feast in your house, and you serve a tasty drink that flows like a river. The life-giving fountain belongs to you, and your light gives light to each of us (Psalm 36:5, 8-9).

Memories

Make a list of the special candles you use during Advent and Christmas, such as those in the Advent wreath, the centerpiece on your table, the ones on your fireplace mantle, or those received on the day of baptism. For each candle identified as a gift, indicate the giver; for each identified as a purchase, indicate the purchaser. Add to this list each year as needed.

Cards

Scripture

God sent the angel Gabriel to the town of Nazareth in Galilee with a message for a virgin named Mary. She was engaged to Joseph from the family of King David. The angel greeted Mary and said, "You are truly blessed! The Lord is with you" (Luke 1:26-28).

Reflection

While we send greetings cards throughout the year to commemorate birthdays, graduations, anniversaries, grandparents' day, Valentine's Day, and Easter, we send the greatest number of cards at Christmas. For some people, the Christmas card becomes a vehicle for an annual letter that sends seasonal greetings and summarizes their lives during the past year.

One of the first Christmas cards was sent by God, delivered by Gabriel, and received by Mary. It contained greetings, well-wishes, and an important statement about God's presence with the young woman of Nazareth. In other words, it accomplished what we try to imitate every time we mail a Christmas card. Our card conveys our greetings, offers expressions of joy to family and friends, and declares that God is with us, that God is Emanuel.

Proclaiming Emanuel, God-with-us, is the purpose of sending a Christmas card, whether it's a "religious" card (portraying images such as Mary and Joseph, the magi, etc.) or a "secular" card (portraying seasonal images such as birds, a decorated home, a fireplace, etc.). The card, delivered by a mail carrier, shares the good news of the presence of God that we have experienced with those we love.

Meditation

How do the Christmas cards you receive bring the presence of God to you from the senders? How do the cards you send do the same?

Prayer

A river and its streams bring joy to the city, which is the sacred home of God Most High. God is in that city. He will help it at dawn. Our God says, "Calm down, and learn that I am God!" The Lord All-Powerful is with us (Psalm 46:4-5, 10-11).

Memories

Make a list of the people you send Christmas cards to this year. Note how many years you have sent a greeting to each person. Modify this list each year as needed.

Cookies

Scripture

> To the widow of Zarephath, Elijah said, "Go home and fix something for you and your son. But first, please make a small piece of bread and bring it to me. The Lord God of Israel has promised that your jar of flour won't run out and your bottle of oil won't dry up before he sends rain for the crops" (1 Kings 17:13-14).

Reflection

Many of us enter into a baking frenzy before Christmas. We prepare and store cookies in all shapes, sizes and tastes. Usually these are unique cookies, baked only during Christmastime and served to enhance the specialness and sacredness of the season. Some of us bake or buy fruitcakes or other tasty treats that fill store shelves and catalogue pages only at this time of the year. Others bake small loaves of sweet breads filled with cranberries, bananas, apples, raisins or other fruits and seeds.

The point of the annual baking frenzy is to prepare food to share with our family, friends and neighbors. We greet those who live around us with a paper plate of cookies or a loaf of sweet bread, dressed in foil or plastic wrap, and sporting a large red or green bow. This is our way of entering into the communion of the season with those we care about.

The prophet Elijah invites the widow of Zarephath to do the same with him. After asking her to share what little she has with him by baking a small loaf of bread, he promises her that she will reap an abundance through her sharing. Isn't that what happens to us when exchange baked goods with family and neighbors at Christmastime?

Meditation

For you, what is the deeper meaning of the sharing of baked goods or other edible items with family and neighbors?

Prayer

Our Lord, by your wisdom you made so many things; the whole earth is covered with your living creatures. All of these depend on you to provide them with food, and you feed each one with your own hand, until they are full. You created all of them by your Spirit, and you give new life to the earth (Psalm 104:24, 27-28, 30).

Memories

Make a list of the names of people to whom you give cookies, breads or other items of food this Christmas. After each name indicate what food item you give. Also make a list of the names of people who give you cookies, breads or other items of food, and indicate what you receive from each person. Be sure to date your entries. Do the same in years to come.

Dove

Scripture

Noah wanted to find out if the water had gone down, and he sent out a dove. Deep water was still everywhere, and the dove could not find a place to land. So it flew back to the boat. Noah held out his hand and helped it back in. Seven days later Noah sent the dove out again. It returned in the evening, holding in its beak a green leaf from an olive tree (Genesis 8:8-11).

Reflection

A white dove makes its appearance at Christmastime as a sign of peace. Small white doves, often made from real feathers, can be found roosting on the branches of Christmas trees in people's homes around the world. The pope usually releases a dove from his window on New Year's Day as a sign of his desire for peace throughout the world in the new year.

There is more to the dove than its meaning as a symbol of hope for world peace, however. The dove is also a sign of the peace that results from God's re-creation of the world. That's what the story of Noah is all about. God remakes the world, and that remaking begins with peace.

That same re-creating can be found in the narrative of Jesus' baptism in the Jordan River by John the Baptist in Mark's Gospel. Jesus is submersed into the water, like the earth is covered in the story of Noah. And like Noah, who survived the flood to begin life again in peace, Jesus emerges from the water and the Holy Spirit alights on him in the form of a dove. In Jesus, God re-creates the world in peace.

Meditation

How does the image of a dove capture or illustrate the peace of the season for you?

Prayer

I wish I had wings like a dove, so I could fly far away and be at peace. I ask for your help, Lord God, and you will keep me safe. O Lord, we belong to you (Psalm 55:6, 16, 22).

Memories

Make a list of the Christmas cards you receive that have pictures of doves on them. Record who sent each card to you and the type of peace that the sender of the card wishes for you. If you have any doves that you use on your tree or wreaths, note where you purchased them or who gave them to you. Add to this list each year as needed.

Dromedary

Scripture

Jerusalem, stand up! Shine! Your new day is dawning. The glory of the lord shines brightly on you. The earth and its people are covered with darkness, but the glory of the Lord is shining upon you. Your country will be covered with caravans of young camels.... The people...will bring gold and spices in praise of me, the Lord (Isaiah 60:1-2, 6).

Reflection

A dromedary is a type of camel that is associated with the Feast of the Epiphany of the Lord, celebrated on the Second Sunday after Christmas in the United States and other countries (on January 6 in some countries). One of the texts read on the Epiphany is from Matthew's Gospel—the story about the magi who are depicted in most Nativity scenes as having ridden camels. However, while the gospel doesn't mention anything about camels, the other text read on the feast, from the prophet Isaiah, does mention camels. For that reason at least one dromedary is found in or around most displays of the Nativity.

For nomadic people living in deserts, such as the Israelites, camels were a source of food, clothing, shelter and transportation. The beasts' ability to store lots of food and water made them ideal for desert existence. Our own experience of the camel is probably limited to what we've seen at zoos.

No matter how camels are portrayed in the creche, Isaiah sees them as bearers of gifts that people need to survive. In other words, camels are the source of life for ancient people. The ancient prophet declares that caravans of camels flow toward Jerusalem and its light in praise of God.

Meditation

Who or what bears life-sustaining gifts to you? To whom do you bring life-sustaining gifts?

Prayer

Long live the king! Give him gold. Let cities overflow with food and hills be covered with grain. Let the people in the cities prosper like wild flowers. May the glory of the king shine brightly forever like the sun in the sky (Psalm 72:15-17).

Memories

Make a list of the gifts you consider to be your most-treasured things received at Christmastime. Note who gave you each gift and the year you received it. Add to this list each year as needed.

Evergreen

Scripture

Don't you know? Haven't you heard? The Lord is the eternal God, Creator of the earth. He never gets weary or tired; his wisdom cannot be measured (Isaiah 40:28).

Reflection

At Christmastime, we see evergreen branches of spruce, cedar, juniper, fir or pine twisted around banisters, hung as garlands around doors and windows, and stretched out on the mantels of fireplaces. The evergreen can be woven into a circle to form a wreath, or its branches can be placed stem-to-stem to make a swatch, topped off with a large red bow in the middle.

Evergreen is part of our Christmas decorations, because it represents the eternity of God. The eternal God willed to become human like us in the person of Jesus of Nazareth. To remind us of God entering into our world in an everlasting, eternal covenant with us, we use evergreen branches—a sign of eternal life.

Because we are finite and think out of a paradigm that everything has a beginning and an end, the concept of God as infinite is impossible for us to comprehend. The evergreen Christmas decorations we enjoy can put us in contact with the everlasting, the "evergreening" God, manifested in the child Jesus.

Meditation

What types of evergreen are used in and around your home to signal eternity and the eternal faithfulness of God? To what aspect of God's eternity does each type lead you?

Prayer

Our Lord, in all generations you have been our home. You have always been God—long before the birth of the mountains, even before you created the earth and the world. Our Lord and our God, treat us with kindness and let all go well for us (Psalm 90:1-2, 17).

Memories

Make a list of the evergreen decorations you have either made or bought for your home to be used this year. Be sure to date your entries. Add to this list each year as needed.

Family

Scripture

I kneel in prayer to the Father. All beings in heaven and on earth receive their life from him. God is wonderful and glorious. I pray that his Spirit will make you become strong followers and that Christ will live in your hearts because of your faith (Ephesians 3:14-17).

Reflection

On the Sunday between Christmas Day and New Year's Day (or December 30 when there is no Sunday), we mark the Feast of the Holy Family. Some time between Thanksgiving Day and New Year's Day most families—including extended families—gather around a common table and, through story-telling and eating and drinking, remember who they are as a family. The exchange of gifts sometimes further enhances their identity as family.

Most likely, some form of ritual is observed at this annual gathering. The ritual might entail gathering in the same place every year, eating foods that are prepared only once a year for this particular meal, playing games that are played year after year, or watching sports events on television. We see these rituals take shape as we listen to the family's candid comments: a grandparent telling a younger member of the family, "That's not the way we do that," parents telling their children, "No, that goes over here," or someone in the kitchen asking, "Where's that platter we always use for the turkey?"

Family rituals are important, because they control the gradual unfolding of the events that give a family its identity. They free the participants to enter into events so that they can leave the gathering with a clearer identity of themselves as a family.

Meditation

What are your family's most important holiday rituals? What identity do your rituals disclose about your family?

Prayer

The Lord will not forget to give us his blessing. All who worship the Lord will receive his blessing. I pray that the Lord will let your family and your descendants always grow strong. May the Lord who created the heavens and the earth give you his blessing (Psalm 115:12-15).

Memories

Make a list of how your family has been changed by births, deaths and marriages during this past year. Do the same each year.

Frankincense

Scripture

When the (wise) men went into the house and saw the child (Jesus) with Mary, his mother, they knelt down and worshipped him. They took out their gifts of gold, frankincense, and myrrh and gave them to him (Matthew 2:11).

Reflection

Frankincense, one of the three gifts brought by the magi to the house where Mary and Jesus are staying after his birth in Bethlehem, is a fragrant gum resin from trees. When mixed with other sweet spices and resins, it can be burned in a fire or on hot coals to give off a pleasant-smelling smoke.

Frankincense is one of the three gifts carried by the magi, and one traditionally given when someone died in the ancient world. By burning it before the deceased is buried, the stench of decaying flesh is covered up. The author of Matthew's Gospel uses this tradition to inform the reader about the fate of the child.

Frankincense is seldom burned in churches and homes—especially in homes that have smoke detectors! Modern equivalents of frankincense are scented candles and potpourri that release an intense aroma, filling a home with food for the nose at Christmastime.

Meditation

For you, what are the smells of Christmas? Identify how each smell is food for your nose.

Prayer

The Lord alone deserves all of the praise, because of his love and faithfulness. Our God is in the heavens, doing as he chooses. The idols of the nations are made of silver and gold. Their noses can't smell. The Lord has kept the heavens for himself, but he has given the earth to us humans. Shout praises to the Lord! (Psalm 115:1, 3, 6, 16, 18).

Memories

Make a list of the smells of Christmas in your home this year. Note the memories you associate with each smell. Modify this list each year as needed.

Gloria

Scripture

Suddenly many...angels came down from heaven and joined in praising God. They said: "Praise God in heaven! Peace on earth to everyone who pleases God" (Luke 2:13-14).

Reflection

"Gloria in excelsis Deo," meaning "Glory to God in the highest," is the song the angels sing in Luke's Gospel after Jesus is born and the shepherds are notified. While the Latin phrase can still be found on a banner held by the angel hanging over a creche, it is also the opening line of a hymn sung at the beginning of Mass. The author of Luke's Gospel repeats the line when Jesus enters Jerusalem riding on a donkey as the crowds shout, "Peace in heaven and glory to God" (Luke 19:38). For Luke, the one who was born is preparing to be born again through death.

"Gloria in excelsis Deo" praises the God who lives above the dome and the waters above the dome of the sky in ancient Hebrew cosmology. It declares that the one God deserves all honor, admiration and praise for the great deed of the incarnation of the Son.

We engage in such praise of God through carols at Christmastime. They waft over the radio air waves and accompany us while we shop. We know their lyrics from memory.

Christmas carols help us recall and retell in song what God has done for us. Like "Gloria in excelsis Deo," carols praise God with song.

Meditation

What is your favorite Christmas carol? What are your favorite lyrics? How do the lyrics of your favorite Christmas carol help you recall and retell the events of Christmas?

Prayer

The heavens keep telling the wonders of God, and the skies declare what he has done. Each day informs the following day; each night announces to the next. They don't speak a word, and there is never the sound of a voice. Yet their message reaches all the earth, and it travels around the world (Psalm 19:1-4).

Memories

Ask each member of your immediate family to name his or her favorite Christmas carol. Record the family member's name and the name of the carol. Modify this list each year as needed.

Gold

Scripture

I will bring bronze and iron in place of wood and stone; in place of bronze and iron, I will bring gold and silver. I will appoint peace and justice as your rulers and leaders (Isaiah 60:17).

Reflection

Gold represents royalty, symbolized by the gold crowns worn by kings and queens for thousands of years. In the ancient world, gold was given to help defray the expenses of burial, and two gold coins were placed over the eyes of the deceased to keep them closed. Today a gold watch speaks of wealth, and gold chains, bracelets, brooches and rings are often given to express a deep and lasting love. As a symbol, gold represents that which is precious.

Gold glistens all around us at Christmastime. It is one of the three gifts brought by the magi to the infant Jesus in Matthew's Gospel, where it serves as a funerary gift. In Epiphany plays, children portraying the magi often wear crowns sparkling with gold glitter. Gold-colored ornaments hang on our tree; gold-colored bells decorate our front door or mantle; gold-colored bows on gifts entice curious youngsters to sneak a peek.

Gold is appropriate for Christmastime—when we celebrate the precious gift of God's Son to the world. The King of Kings comes into our midst, bearing the precious gift of eternal life.

Meditation

Who is the golden person you cherish most at Christmastime? What is precious about this person?

Prayer

Worshipping the Lord is sacred; he will always be worshipped. All of his decisions are correct and fair. They are worth more than the finest gold and are sweeter than honey from a honeycomb (Psalm 19:9-10).

Memories

Make a list of the gold items you wear or display at Christmastime. Next to each item, indicate if it was a purchase or a gift, and where you got it or who gave it to you. Include dates if possible. Modify this list each year as needed.

Holly

Scripture

The soldiers led Jesus inside the courtyard of the fortress and called together the rest of the troops. They put a purple robe on him, and on his head they placed a crown that they had made out of thorn branches (Mark 15:16-17).

Reflection

Holly, a popular Christmas decoration, is a type of tree or shrub with spiny evergreen leaves and red berries. A legend explains why holly berries are red and why they are connected to the passion of Jesus.

According to the legend, a holly tree is growing near the door of the stable where Jesus has been born, but its berries are white, as they are throughout the summer. One person who comes to see the infant Jesus has no gift, so that person breaks off a branch of the holly. When Jesus accepts the holly branch, he pricks his finger on one of its thorns and leaves his blood on the spiny leaves. In grief and embarrassment, the holly berries turn red.

The legend continues by connecting the thorns of the holly leaves and their red berries to the crown of thorns placed on the head of Jesus before his crucifixion. Thus the birth of Jesus and the pricking of his finger are connected to his passion and the shedding of his blood, especially as he is crowned with thorn branches. This shedding-of-blood theme is present at

Christmastime on the Feast of Saint Stephen (December 26), on the Feast of the Holy Innocents (December 28), and on the Memorial of Saint Thomas Becket (December 29).

Meditation

What connections do you make between Christmastime and Eastertime?

Prayer

Our Lord, your mighty power makes the king glad. You did what he wanted most and never told him "No." You truly blessed the king, and you placed on him a crown of finest gold. He asked to live a long time, and you promised him life that never ends (Psalm 21:1-4).

Memories

Make a list of the ways you use holly to decorate your home. Note from where the holly comes. Include in your list any table cloths or scarves with holly patterns on them. Modify this list each year as needed.

*I*nnocents

Scripture

When Herod found out that the wise men from the east had tricked him, he was very angry. He gave orders for his men to kill all the boys who lived in or near Bethlehem and were two years old and younger (Matthew 2:16).

Reflection

Three days after celebrating Christmas, the Church marks the Feast of the Holy Innocents, the observance of a biblical story unique to Matthew's Gospel. The author of this gospel wants to portray Jesus as a type of Moses, who escapes the pharaoh's declaration that every male child born to the Hebrews be thrown into the river and drowned. Thus, Jesus escapes the murderous action of Herod through the flight of his parents with him from Bethlehem to Egypt, from where he will emerge as the liberator of his people.

We often fail to notice the theme of death and resurrection that permeates the season of Christmas. We get so caught up in the joy of Jesus' birth that we don't make a connection to the new birth that awaits us on the other side of the grave. The Church reminds us, however. The day after Christmas we mark the Feast of Saint Stephen's birth into eternal life by stoning. The next day we remember Saint John the Evangelist and read his account of the resurrection, Jesus' birth from death to life. Then the Feast of the Holy Innocents, also celebrating death and everlasting life, is followed by the memory of Thomas

Becket, the twelfth-century Archbishop of Canterbury who was murdered in his cathedral by King Henry II's thugs and born into eternal life.

The interconnectedness of Christmas and the feasts that follow it attempt to tell us that the only way to enter into eternal life is through death. That's why the Church refers to the day of a martyr's death as his or her birthday—a birth into eternal life. Ultimately that's what Jesus teaches through his birth, death and resurrection. He is a holy innocent who is crucified, but God raises him to eternal life. His first birth is paralleled by his second.

Meditation

Who are the holy innocents who are put to death today? How do you think their deaths are their birthdays into eternal life?

Prayer

I wash my hands, Lord, to show my innocence, and I worship at your altar, while gratefully singing about your wonders. I love the temple where you live, and where your glory shines. Don't punish me with death. I stay true to myself. Be kind and rescue me (Psalm 26:6-9, 11).

Memories

Make a list of the names of the members of your family and friends who have died around Christmastime. Record the date of each person's death after his or her name. Add to this list each year as needed.

Jesus

Scripture

The angel said, "Joseph, the baby that Mary will have is from the Holy Spirit. Go ahead and marry her. Then after her baby is born, name him Jesus, because he will save his people from their sins." So the Lord's promise came true, just as the prophet had said, "A virgin will have a baby boy, and he will be called Emanuel," which means "God is with us" (Matthew 1:20-23).

Reflection

Naming is an important exercise; we organize life by naming people, places and things, which helps us identify and understand their functions.

For example, the word "mother" tells us that person's function in relationship to another. We can expect to see a mother nurturing, protecting, and caring for her child. "Dining room" indicates a place for eating. In the dining room we can expect to find that which will facilitate the act of eating. "Light switch" indicates a device that controls the light given off by a lamp. We can expect the light to go on or off when we flip the switch.

A personal name, however, is especially significant. It not only distinguishes a person from all others, but it also describes an individual who is in the ongoing state of development from birth to death. The author of Matthew's Gospel makes this point when he portrays the angel as telling Joseph to name Mary's child Jesus because he will save his people from their sins. The name describes Jesus' role. Matthew further specifies this role by loosely quoting the prophet, Isaiah, and saying that Jesus is God-with-us, Emanuel. This meaning is fully understood at the end of the gospel when Jesus tells his followers that he will be with them always until the end of the world.

Meditation

How does your name describe you? How does it describe your role or ministry or mission in life?

Prayer

I will always praise the Lord. With all my heart, I will praise the Lord. Let all who are helpless, listen and be glad. Honor the Lord with me! Celebrate his great name. Honor the Lord! You are his special people (Psalm 34:1-3, 9).

Memories

Make a list of the names of the members of your family. After each name, explain how you see that person's particular role or ministry or mission. Modify this list each year as needed.

Joachim and Anne

Scripture

From the exile to the birth of Jesus, his ancestors (included) Matthan, Jacob, and Joseph, the husband of Mary, the mother of Jesus, who is called the Messiah (Matthew 1:12, 15-16).

Reflection

It's interesting to note that the author of Matthew's Gospel, who seems to be especially concerned about Jesus' family tree, never mentions Mary's parents. Most people are unaware that their traditional names, Joachim and Anne, come from a non-canonical gospel called The Protevangelium of James. According to the story, Joachim and Anne are advanced in years and have no children. Anne intercedes with God, and an angel of the Lord announces to her that she will conceive and bear a daughter who is destined to serve God all the days of her life.

Joachim, who has been tending his flocks, receives a revelation from an angel as well. He is told that he is going to be a father. Selecting lambs, calves and kids, Joachim makes an offering to God in thanksgiving for the gift God has given to him. Nine months later, Anne gives birth to a daughter. This child is named Mary, and she will become the mother of Jesus, making Joachim and Anne Jesus' grandparents.

Grandparents are important members of any family gathering, especially so at Christmastime and even if it is only in spirit or memory. They represent the generations and the wisdom of our latter years. Grandparents are usually considered to be more accessible to grandchildren than even the children's own parents. When grandparents live a great distance from their children and grandchildren, their presence is especially important at Christmastime and at other family gatherings. If they can't be there in person, there should be lots of phone calls, pictures and videos exchanged. If the grandparents are deceased, it is very meaningful for the family to remember them in special ways at Christmastime.

Meditation

What roles do your parents play in your family gatherings? What roles do/did your grandparents play in your family gatherings when you were young?

Prayer

You are the only God, ruling from your throne and praised by Israel. Our ancestors trusted you, and you rescued them. When they cried out for help, you saved them, and you did not let them down when they depended on you. You, Lord, brought me safely through birth, and you protected me when I was a baby at my mother's breast. From the day I was born, I have been in your care and from the time of my birth, you have been my God (Psalm 22:3-5, 9-10).

Memories

Prepare a family tree showing the two parents, the four grandparents, and the eight great-grandparents on both sides. Display your family tree each holiday season.

Joseph

Scripture

This is how Jesus Christ was born. A young woman named Mary was engaged to Joseph from King David's family. But before they were married, she learned that she was going to have a baby by God's Holy Spirit. Joseph was a good man and did not want to embarrass Mary in front of everyone. So he decided to quietly call off the wedding (Matthew 1:18-19).

Reflection

There is not much mention of Joseph in the canonical gospels, other than in Matthew's Gospel, where he—and not Mary, as in Luke's Gospel—is the recipient of the revelation concerning the birth of Jesus. So few words are devoted to Joseph because he represents a paternity problem for Matthew's Jewish readers. In Jewish understanding, if Joseph isn't the father of Jesus, then Jesus isn't from King David's line. If he is the father of Jesus, then God isn't the child's father, and Mary is not a virgin. The author of Matthew's Gospel solves this problem by appealing to the power of God, who in the past did great deeds and who continues to do them through the birth and death and resurrection of Jesus.

The depiction of Joseph as an old man with a beard and holding a flowering staff in his hand, as can be seen in images of him in creches or statuary, comes from a story in the non-canonical Protevangelium of James. According to the account, Joachim and Anne, the parents of Mary, are rich people. Mary is sent to the Temple when she is two years old and stays there until she is twelve, the time to be married. The priests decide that Mary should be the bride of a widower. Several present their staffs to the priest, who takes them into the Temple, prays for a sign to determine whose wife she should be, and then returns the staffs to their owners. When Joseph receives his staff, a dove comes out of it and flies to his head, a sign that he is to take Mary as his wife. In statuary, the staff Joseph holds has a lily blossoming at the top to represent his purity.

In Matthew's Gospel, Joseph is portrayed as a model of righteousness, a person who does what God wants, even if it means breaking the law. Because Mary is found to be with child, Joseph should present her to the authorities and have her stoned to death. Instead, he breaks the law in order to abide by the revelation from God he receives in a dream. Thus, his righteousness or justice exceeds the law. He does the right thing because it is the right thing to do.

Meditation

Who are some of the people you know who do the right thing because it is the right thing to do, who are upright, just, righteous? What makes them this way?

Prayer

Our Lord, judge me and show that I am honest and innocent. You know every heart and mind, and you always do right. You, God, are my shield, the protector of everyone whose heart is right. You see that justice is done. I will praise you, Lord! You always do right (Psalm 7:8-11, 17).

Memories

Make a list of members of your family and friends who are named Joseph. Identify how each Joseph represents uprightness, justice and righteousness. Modify this list each year as needed.

Kings

Scripture

When Jesus was born in the village of Bethlehem in Judea, Herod was king. During this time some wise men from the east came to Jerusalem and said, "Where is the child born to be king of the Jews? We saw his star in the east and have come to worship him" (Matthew 2:1-2).

Reflection

Although we often see them depicted with crowns on their heads, the wise men, or magi, are not kings, according to the text in Matthew's Gospel. In fact, by making them kings, the tension in the story between Herod the king and Jesus the king is lost. The attribute of kingship comes from Psalm 72:10, which is used as a Responsorial Psalm on the Feast of the Epiphany. This Scripture mentions the kings of Sheba and Seba bringing gifts.

Traditionally named Melchior, Balthasar and Caspar, the three wise men statues portray two white men and one black man offering gifts to the infant Jesus. The portrayal of *three* persons comes from the three funerary gifts of gold, frankincense and myrrh, which they bring to present to Jesus. Matthew's text doesn't mention the number of magi or their names. Popular tradition, as best seen in the Christmas carol "We Three Kings," has brought that about through the ages.

The desire to attribute royalty to the magi can serve to represent the inherent dignity of every human being. By the fact of our birth, we are royal in God's eyes. We are graced with God's gift of self and recognize that same gift in others. That is why we reach outward at Christmastime to those who are more needy than we are. From the depths of our royal neediness, we offer food, money, clothing and shelter to those regal people who have little or none. Thus we not only acknowledge the human dignity of others but discover that our own is enhanced through our generosity.

Meditation

Whose human dignity have you recently enhanced? How did you make that person feel like royalty? Who recently enhanced your human dignity? How did he or she make you feel like royalty?

Prayer

Our Lord, you will always rule. You listen to the longing of those who suffer. You offer them hope, and you pay attention to their cries for help. You defend orphans and everyone else in need (Psalm 10:16-18).

Memories

Make a list of the organizations to which you and the other members of your family volunteer time, talent or treasure at Christmastime. Next to each person's name indicate what specific gift that person offers. Be sure to date your entries. Modify this list each year as needed.

Lucy

Scripture

You are like light for the whole world. A city built on top of a hill cannot be hidden, and no one would light a lamp and put it under a clay pot. A lamp is placed on a lampstand, where it can give light to everyone in the house. Make your light shine, so that others will see the good that you do and will praise your Father in heaven (Matthew 5:14-16).

Reflection

We mark the Memorial of Saint Lucy on December 13. Her name means "light," which is why she is usually pictured with a crown of burning candles on her head.

In legend, Lucy is born of noble parents in Sicily. As a young woman, she refuses marriage to a suitor and prefers a life of virginity. During the fourth-century reign of Emperor Diocletian, Lucy's suitor denounces her as a Christian and has her sentenced to a brothel. When soldiers are unable to move her from her home, however, she is ordered burned at the stake, but the flames don't touch her. Finally she is stabbed, dying a martyr for her faith. Thus Lucy is like a light for the whole world, both in name and in action.

At Christmastime many people decorate both the inside and the outside of the their homes with lights. Inside, the lights are found on the tree, hung in windows or around doors, and intertwined with garland on the fireplace. Outside, the lights outline rooftops or the branches of trees or shrubs. When the lights are turned on, our homes cannot be hidden—inside or outside.

Like Lucy, we are exhorted to make the light of our faith shine like the inside and outside of our homes at Christmastime. We are called to put into action what we express with our lips. We do this not for our own aggrandizement but so that others will desire to participate in the good they see. In this way, God—the source of all light—is praised.

Meditation

How does your light shine both inside and outside during Advent and Christmas?

Prayer

You are always loyal to your loyal people, and you are faithful to the faithful. With all who are sincere, you are sincere. You, the Lord God, keep my lamp burning and turn darkness to light. Your way is perfect, Lord, and your word is correct. You are a shield for those who run to you for help. You alone are God! (Psalm 18:25-26, 28, 30-31).

Memories

Record a description of how you have decorated your home with lights for the past several years and for this year. Be sure to date your entries. Do this in years to come.

Manger

Scripture

The shepherds were frightened. But the angel said, "Don't be afraid! I have good news for you, which will make everyone happy. This very day in King David's hometown a Savior has been born for you. He is Christ the Lord. You will know who he is, because you will find him dressed in baby clothes and lying on a bed of hay" (Luke 2:9-12).

Reflection

The bed of straw for the infant Jesus serves as a manger, an open box holding feed, fodder or hay for livestock. Most scenes of the Nativity depict the infant Jesus nestled in such a box, filled with straw, Mary and Joseph kneeling or standing on either side.

Luke portrays Jesus in a feeding trough because he considers Jesus to be food for people. In no other gospel is Jesus portrayed as eating so many meals with people both before and after his death. In the process of eating, Jesus gives himself as sustenance through word and food.

We do the same, especially at Christmastime when families gather around tables laden with ham or turkey, sweet or mashed potatoes, green beans and other vegetables, dressing and gravy, sweet breads, pies, and cookies. The table is our manger. As we share stories of people and experiences that have given meaning to our lives, we pass around the food—and as we do, we pass around one another. As we spoon or ladle or spear food from a common bowl or plate, we feast on one another. We are filled with life from the manger, otherwise known as our own dining room table.

Meditation

In what ways are you food for others? How have others been food for you?

Prayer

Our Lord, by your wisdom you made so many things; the whole earth is covered with your living creatures. All of these depend on you to provide them with food, and you feed each one with your own hand, until they are full. You created all of them by your Spirit, and you give new life to the earth (Psalm 104:24, 27-28, 30).

Memories

Make a list of the items that were on your table-manger last Christmas. Record both last year's and this year's menu, and date your entries. Do the same in years to come.

Mary

Scripture

The apostles often met together and prayed with a single purpose in mind. The women and Mary the mother of Jesus would meet with them, and so would his brothers (Acts 1:14).

Reflection

Mary, a modern spelling of Miriam, Moses' sister's name, is hailed as the Mother of God on January 1. Artistic expressions of Mary usually portray her as a young teenage girl sitting or standing by the infant Jesus, wearing blue and white.

We often forget, however, that Mary continues in faithfulness to God long after Jesus is born and long after he is crucified, dies, and is raised to new life. Luke's Acts of the Apostles reminds us that Mary could be found praying with Jesus' first followers. Prayer is a thread woven throughout her life, a means whereby she not so much talks to God but listens to God's plan for her. In her prayer, Mary is a model for us in God's presence, especially at Christmastime. In her we see how God works through people. God overwhelms us with the divine Spirit, impregnating us with the fullness of life and enabling us to bring life to others.

Like Mary during her pregnancy, we too must wait. We must not be too anxious to have everything the minute we think we deserve it. We must wait while we grow, like Jesus' mother waited for him to mature into a young man. Even in our older years, like Mary, we are to wait in prayer for God to act in our lives.

Meditation

What new life or what birth has God's Spirit brought forth from you recently? How long did you wait for God to act?

Prayer

With all my heart, I am waiting, Lord for you! I trust your promises. I wait for you more eagerly than a solider on guard duty waits for the dawn. Yes, I wait more eagerly than a soldier on guard duty waits for the dawn (Psalm 130:5-6).

Memories

Make a list of the people and events you waited for last year at Christmastime. Make a list of the people and events you wait for this year at Christmastime. Do the same in years to come.

Myrrh

Scripture

When the (wise) men went into the house and saw the child with Mary, his mother, they knelt down and worshipped him. They took out their gifts of gold, frankincense, and myrrh and gave them to him (Matthew 2:11).

Reflection

Myrrh is a sweet-smelling perfume used to anoint the body. According to Matthew's Gospel, it is one of the gifts the magi brought to the infant Jesus. Although the ancient world used it to anoint the living, myrrh was primarily reserved as an ointment to cover the stench of death. Myrrh could fill a whole house with its aroma. Today myrrh might be considered as a perfume, an aftershave, or a deodorant. Even though we wear certain artificial scents, every person has a natural, unique, and discernible fragrance, like that of a new baby or one's grandmother, parent or sibling.

Many of us associate Christmastime with specific smells, such as the sap from pine, fir or spruce; musty hay in the creche; strawberry-scented candles on the table; certain cooking odors; the smell of wood burning in the fireplace. Seasonal aromas brought into our homes are a delight for our noses.

Besides the scents of Christmas, however, there is also the fragrance that is innate to our house. Who can't remember the smell of their grandparents' home, the mustiness that wafts between the book-laden shelves of a library, the malodor of formaldehyde in a high school laboratory, or the disinfectant scent in hospital corridors and rooms? Each of these smells connects us to a past experience and enables us to recall its significance in our lives.

Reflection

What is your favorite perfume or aftershave? Describe its scent. In what ways do you consider that scent a gift to others?

Prayer

You are God, and you will rule forever as king. Your royal power brings about justice. You love justice and hate evil. And so, your God chose you and made you happier than any of your friends. The sweet aroma of the spices of myrrh, aloes, and cassia, covers your royal robes (Psalm 45:6-8).

Memories

Make a list of the significant people in your life, living or deceased. Next to each name make a note about that person's natural, unique scent and the smell of that person's home. Also note what in your home resembles those fragrances. Modify this list each year as needed.

Nativity

Scripture

Mary was engaged to Joseph and traveled with him to Bethlehem. She was soon going to have a baby, and while they were there, she gave birth to her first-born son. She dressed him in baby clothes and laid him on a bed of hay, because there was no room for them in the inn (Luke 2:5-7).

Reflection

We often refer to Christmas as "the Nativity," from the Latin *nasci*, meaning "to be born." The author of Luke's Gospel depicts the circumstances surrounding Jesus' birth using the elements of an engagement, a trip, and the lack of a motel room. Works of art will portray Jesus' Nativity with statues of Mary sitting or kneeling, Joseph standing, and Jesus lying in a manger in a cave or barn in imitation of Luke's narrative. This scene is often called a "creche."

Nasci is the basis for other words, such as "native," indicating one who belongs to a particular place by birth; "national," indicating a person who belongs to a nation or country; and "nature," the inherent character of a person. Each of these words has their respective derivatives, such as "nativeness" or "nativism," "nationalist" or "nationalize," "natural" or "naturalist." All specify or define some aspect of birth.

The birth of Jesus in Luke's Gospel, traditionally portrayed as taking place in a cave, has been used by the author to prefigure Jesus' second birth from the tomb. While at first glance the tomb looks like a place of death, it is really a womb, a place where life is conceived and from which Jesus is born into resurrected life. Thus, Christmas is a mini-Easter, reminding us that we are born not just once but many times throughout our lives as we prepare for our birth into eternal life.

Meditation

What details do you know about the day of your birth—such as place, time, day of the week, etc.? What do you consider to be other major "birth" experiences that you have had?

Prayer

You, Lord, brought me safely through birth, and you protected me when I was a baby at my mother's breast. From the day I was born, I have been in your care, and from the time of my birth, you have been my God (Psalm 22:9-10).

Memories

Describe each nativity scene you display inside or outside your home. Note where you place it, where you got it, and how long you have had it. Modify this list each year as needed.

Nicholas

Scripture

A poor widow came up and put in (the offering box) two coins that were worth only a few pennies. Jesus told his disciples..."I tell you that this poor widow has put in more than all the others. Everyone else gave what they didn't need. But she is very poor and gave everything she had" (Mark 12:42-44).

Reflection

Every year on December 6 we remember Saint Nicholas, a fourth-century bishop of Myra who, after being born of wealthy parents, lives his life giving away his wealth to the poor. According to legend, Nicholas tosses three bags of gold into the house of a father who is about to sell his daughters as prostitutes because he can't afford a dowry for them to marry. He also saves three men who are condemned to death, a fate he himself does not escape during the persecution of Christians under the Emperor Diocletian. Nicholas dies a martyr, which explains why he is pictured dressed in red episcopal vestments.

Through the centuries, Saint Nicholas has come to be called Santa Claus, and his episcopal vesture has become a red suit trimmed in white, banded by a large black belt. Of course, the three bags of gold he gives to the father of three daughters has become his large bag filled with toys waiting to be placed in stockings hung on the mantel of the fireplace.

Today Nicholas' care for the poor is overshadowed by the consumerism that has created an "I want list" by children at Christmastime.

The life of Saint Nicholas reminds us that, no matter how much we have, we are all poor in some way. Some of us are poor in terms of money, food, clothing, shelter. Some of us are poor in terms of relationships, education, abilities, skills. Some of us can't read or write, much less operate a computer.

Poverty, no matter what its degree, is a human equalizer. It is only out of our poverty, like the poor widow in Mark's Gospel, that we find our real riches. That's the legacy Saint Nicholas leaves us.

Meditation

Out of what aspect of your poverty have you discovered riches? What is your wealth?

Prayer

> *I asked the Lord for help, and he saved me from all my fears. Keep your eyes on the Lord! You will shine like the sun and never blush with shame. I was a nobody, but I prayed, and the Lord saved me from all my troubles (Psalm 34:4-6).*

Memories

Record how you have celebrated Saint Nicholas' Day in past years. Date your entries. If you haven't celebrated the saint's feast day, make a list of what you can do this year to show your solidarity with the poor of the world. Modify this list each year as needed.

Ornaments

Scripture

> The Lord said to Moses: "Tell the people to build a chest of acacia wood forty-five inches long, twenty-seven inches wide, and twenty-seven inches high. Cover it inside and out with pure gold and put a gold edging around the lid. When I give you the Ten Commandments written on two flat stones, put them inside the chest" (Exodus 25:10-11, 16).

Reflection

The chest that God tells Moses to instruct the craftspeople to make comes to be known as the Ark of the Covenant. God's throne is considered to be above it, so that when the people carry the box with them they are assured that God is with them and presiding over them. The chest serves as an ornament for the tablets of the law.

The idea of ornaments began as real fruit—apples and oranges—hung on the branches of trees using strips of ribbons. It didn't take artisans long, however, to expand this idea to today's vast array of ornaments of every shape, size and symbol. With the passing of years, many of our ornaments have become family heirlooms—treasures carefully unwrapped, displayed for a few weeks, and then delicately stored away again until next Christmas.

We also adorn ourselves with ornaments, especially over the Christmas and New Year holidays. We wear things like rings, watches, combs, pins, brooches and bracelets, each one representing our unique personalities, our sacred character as people in whom God has chosen to dwell through the birth of Jesus.

Meditation

What items do you use to "ornament" yourself? What aspect of your uniqueness does each ornament represent? In what ways do you experience God dwelling within you?

Prayer

We heard that the sacred chest was somewhere near. Then we said, "Let's go to the throne of the Lord and worship at his feet." Come to your new home, Lord, you and the sacred chest with all of its power (Psalm 132:6-8).

Memories

As you unwrap your Christmas ornaments, inventory each one, and indicate if you bought it or if it was a gift. If it was a gift, note the giver's name. Date each entry as best as you can remember. Add to this list each year as needed.

Poinsettia

Scripture

Boaz married Ruth, and the Lord blessed her with a son. The neighborhood women named him Obed.... When Obed grew up, he had a son named Jesse, who later became the father of King David (Ruth 4:13, 17).

Reflection

The red poinsettia is often associated with Christmas. Most people do not realize that it is not a winter flower at all, however, but a plant that blooms in the summer in Mexico and South America. In the northern hemisphere, the poinsettia is forced to grow in greenhouses. Its red blossoms (called "involucral bracts") around yellow flowers are really its top leaves whose chlorophyll changes from green to red when sparked by longer days of sunshine. Poinsettias are associated with Christmas because of their red leaves and because of the feasts of Saint Stephen, the Holy Innocents, and Saint Thomas Becket—all martyrs who shed their blood for their faith.

During the latter days of Advent, we often hear the hymn, "Behold a Rose of Judah." The hymn uses the imagery of a rose bush and refers to "Jesse's lineage" and the fact that "it came a flower bright / Amid the cold of winter." As the lyrics unfold, we become aware that the "rose" is Jesus. Sometimes this song, based on Isaiah 11:1 ("Like a branch that sprouts from a stump, someone from David's family will someday be king"), is sung after a Jesse tree is decorated with small characters from the Hebrew Bible and a single rose, representing Jesus, is placed at the top.

Poinsettias represent our own flowering, our own blossoming in God's sight. Like Jesus' ancestors traced to Ruth, King David's great-grandmother, we are people who have grown and bloomed in God's sight. We are now about our own growing and blooming—and preparing others to do the same.

Meditation

Who are the people you have helped to grow and bloom? Who helped you to grow and bloom?

Prayer

Just as parents are kind to their children, the Lord is kind to all who worship him, because he knows we are made of dust. We humans are like grass or wild flowers that quickly bloom. But a scorching wind blows, and they quickly wither to be forever forgotten. The Lord is always kind to those who worship him, and he keeps his promises to their descendants who faithfully obey him (Psalm 103:13-18).

Memories

Make a list of the different kinds of flowers that you use to decorate your home this Christmastime. Do the same in years to come.

Quirinius

Scripture

> *About that time Emperor Augustus gave orders for the names of all the people to be listed in record books. These first records were made when Quirinius was governor of Syria. Everyone had to go to their own hometown to be listed (Luke 2:1-3).*

Reflection

Of the four gospel writers, Luke alone situates the birth of Jesus in real time by naming the reigning emperor and governor. The author of Luke's Gospel portrays Joseph and Mary traveling from Galilee to Bethlehem, where Jesus is born. For Luke, it is important that Jesus be born in David's hometown, Bethlehem, even though Jesus is known historically as Jesus of Nazareth.

Luke's inaccuracy is spelled out further when we discover that Quirinius' census takes place several years after Jesus' birth. Our own historical records indicate that Quirinius is not governor of Syria at the time Jesus is born and so, of course, does not order a census at that time. Such incorrect history does not negate Luke's point: Jesus is born into a world ruled by people representing a number of different levels of government.

While we no longer refer to our leaders as emperors, we do live in a world "governed" by presidents, prime ministers, kings, queens, governors, senators, representatives. People in these positions influence our lives and position us in a given time and place in history, like Luke does when writing about Jesus.

Meditation

Identify one way the president, governor, or a local public leader has influenced your life.

Prayer

God goes up to his throne, as people shout and trumpets blast. Sing praise to God our King, the ruler of all the earth! Praise God with songs. God rules the nations from his sacred throne (Psalm 47:5-8).

Memories

Make a list of the names of the people in your family. Next to each name, note who the President of the United States was when that person was born. Also note any other major historical events that took place during that year. In the years to come, note who is president and list all events that mark each year as historical.

Ray

Scripture

Balaam said: "What I saw in my vision hasn't happened yet. But someday, a king of Israel will appear like a star" (Numbers 24:17).

Reflection

If you drive across Kansas and the high plains of Colorado at Christmastime, you'll notice a huge five-pointed star atop most of the grain silos. Strings of lights are attached to some of these stars, representing the stars' rays.

Many of us place stars on top of our Christmas trees or suspend them over a Nativity scene. Some of the stars in our homes are family heirlooms or gifts from special people. No matter where we see a star, it serves as a signal; it draws us to itself and then, using its rays, it points us to others and to Jesus.

Balaam's words in the Hebrew Bible's Book of Numbers inspire the author of Matthew's Gospel in the Christian Bible to write a story about magi following a star to Jerusalem and then to Bethlehem, where they find the infant Jesus—the real star they are seeking. Continuing to take his cue from Balaam, Matthew portrays Jesus as the King of Israel, baby royalty who shakes up King Herod and all of Jerusalem. But the rays of the star don't lead the wise men to powerful Herod; rather, the star's rays lead them to a powerless child, a rising star who, as the story unfolds, will bring new light to the world.

The stars of Christmas are meant to guide us to others and to Jesus. Sometimes we discover, like the magi, that the star is a person who has helped us, supported us, comforted us. That person not only led us, but he or she shed light upon us.

Meditation

Who has been like a star in your life? In what ways did that person guide or help you and shed light upon you?

Prayer

Shout praises to the Lord! Shout the Lord's praises in the highest heavens. Sun and moon, and all of you bright stars, come and offer praise. Let all things praise the name of the Lord (Psalm 148: 1, 3, 5).

Memories

Make a list of all the star-shaped ornaments you use to decorate your home during Christmastime. Note the year you acquired each star and where you purchased it or the name of the person who gave it to you. Note what each star represents or means to you. Add to this list each year as needed.

Redeemer

Scripture

The prophet Anna was...there in the temple. And now she was eighty-four years old. Night and day she served God in the temple by praying and often going without eating. At that time Anna came in and praised God. She spoke about the child Jesus to everyone who hoped for Jerusalem to be set free (Luke 2:36-38).

Reflection

A "redeemer" is one who buys, repurchases or wins back someone or something and frees him, her or it from harm or distress. We call Jesus our Redeemer because he ransoms us from our path away from God, showing us the way to God through his death and resurrection.

At Christmastime we celebrate the beginning of the life of the Redeemer and the beginning of our redemption by gazing through the lens of resurrection. This is what the author of Luke's Gospel does in portraying Anna as an old woman who speaks of Jesus as the one who would set Jerusalem free. Of course, Jesus does not redeem the holy city from the Roman occupation forces, but he does free its inhabitants from all that keeps them from following God.

During Christmastime we remember that Jesus has already redeemed us and set us free—something we could not do for ourselves. God, who has a long history of saving people, decides to reorient us through the birth, teaching, death and resurrection of God's own Son, Jesus. Our role as ransomed people is to share our hope with others, like Anna, even as they share their hope with us.

Meditation

What holds you down? From what do you need redemption? Who might be able to help you?

Prayer

Wake up! Do something, Lord! Why are you sleeping? Don't desert us forever. Why do you keep looking away? Don't forget our sufferings and all of our troubles. We are flat on the ground, holding on to the dust. Do something! Help us! Show how kind you are and come to our rescue (Psalm 44:23-26).

Memories

Make a list of those who have redeemed you during the hustle and bustle of the holidays. Note how each person has rescued or ransomed you. Do the same in years to come.

Reindeer

Scripture

The blind will see, and the ears of the deaf will be healed. Those who were lame will leap around like deer; tongues once silent will begin to shout. Water will rush through the desert. A good road will be there, and it will be named "God's Sacred Highway." It will be for God's people (Isaiah 35:5-6, 8).

Reflection

We know nine of them by name: Dasher, Dancer, Prancer, Vixen, Comet, Cupid, Donder, Blitzen and Rudolph—the red-nosed one—because they are associated with Santa Claus and his flying sleigh. But did you know that Santa's reindeer are also called caribou, creatures that migrate in large herds every year through the Alaskan tundra in search of food and water and a place to rear their young?

Representations of reindeer are popular Christmas decorations. Some reindeer are made of grape vines and sport red bows around their necks. Some are made of metal wires and are wrapped in lights and spaced across lawns. Sometimes the reindeer stand alone; sometimes they are hitched to a sleigh carrying a figure of Santa Claus.

We can fail to see the Christian motif of journey in this type of secular Christmas display. We are pilgrim people on our way to the fullness of life. While we are merely passing through this world, most likely riding in a car or a mini-van rather than a sleigh, we are nonetheless headed down God's good road, prepared for us by the birth and mission of Jesus.

Meditation

Where are you going in your relationship with God? What do you hunger and thirst for at Christmastime?

Prayer

As a deer gets thirsty for streams of water, I truly am thirsty for you, my God. In my heart, I am thirsty for you, the living God. When will I see your face? (Psalm 42:1-2).

Memories

Make a list of the various types of reindeer figures you display as part of your Christmas decorations. Note how and when you acquired each figure, and how it reminds you that you are on a journey to God. If you don't have any reindeer figures, make a list of the ways your thirst for God is satisfied at Christmastime. Modify this list each year as needed.

Shepherds and Sheep

Scripture

In the fields near Bethlehem some shepherds were guarding their sheep. All at once an angel came down to them from the Lord, and the brightness of the Lord's glory flashed around them. After the angels had left and gone back to heaven, the shepherds...hurried off and found Mary and Joseph, and they saw the baby lying on a bed of hay (Luke 2: 8-9, 15-16).

Reflection

Figures of shepherds and sheep are found in most Nativity scenes. Our romantic view of shepherds, however, as gentle people with lambs over their shoulders, whose only purpose in life is to care for the pure, white, cuddly and helpless infant sheep contrasts sharply with the historical reality of shepherds and sheep of the first century.

Shepherds are considered outcasts and thieves in those times. They spend their time as nomads who don't have access to daily baths. Thus they smell like the sheep they look after. Because they pasture their sheep on property belonging to other people, they steal valuable grass. They spend their entire lives with some of the dumbest of animals—sheep—and thus are considered to be much like the flocks they tend.

Luke places shepherds and sheep in his Nativity scene. They represent the poor and the outcast for whom Jesus will serve as shepherd. The Johannine Jesus is portrayed as saying, "I am the good shepherd" (John 10:11). No one considers a shepherd "good" in the ancient world.

Although we are far removed from shepherds and their sheep, they speak to us as Christians in today's world. Each of us is called to be both sheep and shepherd. There are times when our weaknesses leave us helpless, needing to be led and cared for—like sheep. Then there are times when our strengths allow us to be strong and wise, capable of leading others—like shepherds.

Meditation

When have you been a sheep? Who served as your shepherd? When have you been a shepherd? Who was your sheep?

Prayer

You, Lord, are my shepherd. I will never be in need. You let me rest in fields of green grass. You lead me to streams of peaceful water, and you refresh my life. Your kindness and your love will always be with me each day of my life, and I will live forever in your house, Lord (Psalm 23:1-3, 6).

Memories

Note how many shepherds and sheep are depicted in your Nativity scenes and describe each one. Date your entry. Add one shepherd or one or two sheep to a creche this year. Do this in years to come, until you have acquired several shepherds and a whole flock of sheep.

Snow

Scripture

I saw seven gold lampstands. There with the lampstands was someone who seemed to be the Son of Man. He was wearing a robe that reached down to his feet, and a gold cloth was wrapped around his chest. His head and his hair were white as wool or snow, and his eyes looked like flames of fire (Revelation 1:12-14).

Reflection

The Christian Bible's two descriptions of the birth of Jesus (Matthew and Luke) make no mention of snow falling. That hasn't stopped popular piety, however, from adding snow to the depiction of the scene and to the lyrics of Christmas carols. Many of us create the effect of a white Christmas by placing strips of cotton on top of the creche, where the Holy Family seems to take shelter from the harsh winter elements.

Maybe our penchant for snow at Christmastime comes from its freshness, newness and purity. After a snowfall, we discover that a world of brown grass, dead leaves, dusty streets and littered parking lots has been transformed into a bright, pure winter wonderland. We find ourselves stepping out into a new world, a new creation. We can't help but feel our spirits soar as we romp with delight in the play that we can only enjoy when it snows.

From one perspective, that's why snow is associated with Christmas and the white hair of the Son of Man in the Book of

Revelation. The Son of Man, Jesus risen from the dead, is fresh and new and pure. The one who was dead is alive. He represents the new creation, which is exactly what we celebrate at Christmastime. His purity is like a snowfall that covers us with a blanket of white.

Meditation

What does snow mean to you? Besides purity and transformation, what other connections can you make between the beauty of snow and the joy of Christ's birth?

Prayer

As soon as God speaks, the earth obeys. He covers the ground with snow like a blanket of wool, and he scatters frost like ashes on the ground. God sends down hailstones like chips of rocks. Who can stand the cold? At his command the ice melts, the wind blows, and streams begin to flow (Psalm 147:15-18).

Memories

Make a list of the years you experienced a "white" Christmas. Note all the memories you associate with each one. Make a list of the years when you experienced a sunny Christmas. Note all the memories you associate with each one. Make note of what the weather is like on Christmas Day in the years to come.

Tree

Scripture

The angel showed me a river that was crystal clear, and its waters gave life. The river came from the throne where God and the Lamb were seated. Then it flowed down the middle of the city's main street. On each side of the river are trees that grow a different kind of fruit each month of the year. The fruit gives life, and the leaves are used as medicine to heal the nations (Revelation 22:1-2).

Reflection

Most of us bring trees into our homes and decorate them at Christmastime. Some of us go to tree farms, search through the rows of evergreens, and cut the one we like the best. Some of us go to a dealer who lets us pick from a display of already-cut evergreens. Because some of us are allergic to the sap or the smell of evergreen, or because we are ecologically conscious, we simply go to the garage or attic to get our artificial tree out of storage—the same tree we've used for years.

Christmas trees represent the Tree of Life in the Garden of Eden, as described in the second story of creation in the Hebrew Bible's Book of Genesis. The man and woman in the garden never eat of the Tree of Life. Instead, they choose to eat of the Tree of the Knowledge of Good and Evil and thus become like God. Mythologically, if they had eaten of the Tree of Life, they would have lived forever.

The author of the Christian Bible's Book of Revelation portrays the restoration of the Tree of Life in its description of the stream of grace flowing from God to the city where people live. Through the conquest of the Lamb, there is not a single Tree of Life but many trees that produce a different type of fruit for each month of the year. People who eat the fruit receive God's life. Even the leaves of the trees contain God's healing power. Thus paradise is restored. Every Christmas we bring a little bit of that paradise into our homes when we decorate our tree.

Meditation

How does your Christmas tree serve as a sign of God's life for you and your family?

Prayer

Tell the heavens and the earth to be glad and celebrate! Command the ocean to roar with all of its creatures and the fields to rejoice with all of their crops. Then every tree in the forest will sing joyful songs to the Lord. He is coming to judge all people on earth with fairness and truth (Psalm 96:11-12).

Memories

Make a list of the types of trees that you have had for Christmas over the past five years. Date each entry and describe how each tree was decorated and who decorated it. Do the same in years to come.

Urn

Scripture

Now God is shining in our hearts to let you know that his glory is seen in Jesus Christ. We are like clay jars in which this treasure is stored. The real power comes from God and not from us (2 Corinthians 4:6-7).

Reflection

Most people define an urn as a container for ashes or cremated remains. They picture a buried or stored vase-like vessel holding a person's ashes. Besides this use, however, an urn can serve as an object of art, such as the famous Greek pottery urn with the athletes on it.

When providing drink for a large group of people, such as a gathering at Christmastime, a silver urn with a tap and a heating device is often used for coffee, tea or hot water. From this urn, many cups are filled, making it a source of unity for those who are gathered. People discover their unity when they draw sustenance from a common source. Thus the urn has the ability to unite people, just as food does when many share from the same table.

As Paul tells the Corinthians, each one of us is an urn, a vessel, a container in which God's glory—Jesus Christ—is stored. Traditionally understood, that means that we are created in the image and likeness of God. Jesus, in whom dwells the full divinity of God and the full humanity of people, is our model, a treasure we hold in clay urns. Through us, God's glory flashes, like it does in Jesus—and like it does in the unity experienced when people share who they are with one another through drink and food during the Christmas season.

Meditation

How have you experienced yourself being a treasure, a source of God's glory and unity for others?

Prayer

Sing a new song to the Lord! Everyone on this earth, sing praises to the Lord, sing and praise his name. Day after day announce, "The Lord has saved us!" Tell every nation on earth, "The Lord is wonderful, and does marvelous things! The Lord is great and deserves our greatest praise! He is the only God worthy of our worship. Give honor and praise to the Lord, whose power and beauty fill his holy temple" (Psalm 96:1-4, 6).

Memories

If you have an urn of some kind, record where it came from and how you use it, especially at Christmastime. If you don't have an urn, record the types of vessels you use at Christmastime to help family and guests recognize their unity. Add to this record in years to come.

Valley

Scripture

Someone is shouting: "Clear a path in the desert! Make a straight road for the lord our God. Fill in the valleys; flatten every hill and mountain. Level the rough and rugged ground. Then the glory of the Lord will appear for all to see. The Lord has promised this!" (Isaiah 40:3-5).

Reflection

A valley is the territory between mountains or hills. A valley is formed by the erosion of the earth, caused by a river or stream wearing away the surrounding soil. When we stand in a valley, we often see the mountains or hills on either side and a river or stream winding down the center. Because they are easier to cross, valleys are good locations for roads, especially in mountainous states like Colorado, Wyoming and Montana.

The prophet Isaiah offers encouragement to the people of Israel by employing the image of a valley. He tells them that they will leave their Babylonian captivity and will travel on straight roads through the filled-in mountain valleys as they return to Israel and the holy city, Jerusalem. By using this image of an easy walk back home, Isaiah promises the people that God, whose absence they experience in a foreign country, will be with them when they make it back home.

During Advent we hear the words of the prophet Isaiah on the lips of John the Baptist. The leveled-mountain valleys John speaks about are personal. The Baptist knows that from down in the valley it is impossible to see where we are going. So during Advent, he calls us to level the mountains of self-absorption and straighten the roads of selfishness that get in the way of Christmas, the feast of the appearance of the glory of God. Even during Christmastime we may need a little valley-filling as post-holiday depression and stress cause us to sink back to the valley out of which God has called us.

Meditation

What valley in your life needs to be filled so that you can see the glory of God?

Prayer

You are true to your name, and you lead me along the right paths. I may walk through valleys as dark as death, but I won't be afraid. You are with me, and your shepherd's rod makes me feel safe. Your kindness and love will always be with me each day of my life (Psalm 23:3-4, 6).

Memories

Make a list of the valleys you have filled for yourself and your family during the past year. Note the major obstacles you have overcome this year. Date your entries. Add to this list each year as needed.

Winter Solstice

Scripture

Those who walked in the dark have seen a bright light. And it shines upon everyone who lives in the land of darkest shadows. A child has been born for us. We have been given a son who will be our ruler. His names will be Wonderful Advisor and Mighty God, Eternal Father and Prince of Peace (Isaiah 9:2, 6).

Reflection

In the Northern Hemisphere of the third planet from the sun, December 22 marks the shortest day of the year and the longest night, called the Winter Solstice. The darkness that has increased since the Fall Equinox reaches its crescendo this day, and the daylight hours begin to lengthen, heading toward the Spring Equinox. It is no wonder that we find ourselves preoccupied with light—candles, lights on trees, lights outside our homes, fires in fireplaces—as darkness reigns.

We are drawn to the light, like moths circling a lamp. In our desire to light up the darkness, however, we can miss the holiness of the night. Dark is not to be equated with evil. On the contrary, we actually can "see" others much better in the dark! In the dark we feel secure enough to share our deepest thoughts and enter into intimacy others. People make love in the dark. People pray in the dark corners of their homes and churches.

It comes as no surprise then, that Christians mark the birth of Jesus, the bright light shining in a dark world, during the darkness of winter. The old Roman feast in honor of the unconquerable sun, that began to grow brighter by December 25, was replaced with the feast of the unconquerable Son, whose resurrection spread eternal light throughout the universe. It is no accident that Jesus' birth, like his resurrection from the dead, traditionally is celebrated in the middle of the night. It is easier to see the light when we are bathed in darkness.

Meditation

What experiences have you had of "seeing" others better in the dark? In what ways did their light scatter some of your darkness?

Prayer

Shout praises to the Lord! The Lord blesses everyone who worships him and gladly obeys his teachings. Their descendants will have great power in the land, because the Lord blesses all who do right. They will be so kind and merciful and good, that they will be a light in the dark for others who do the right thing (Psalm 112:1-2, 4).

Memories

Make a list of the ways you use light to scatter darkness during Christmastime in your own home. Add to this list each year as needed.

Wreath

Scripture

"Everyone who drinks this water will get thirsty again. But no one who drinks the water I give will ever be thirsty again. The water I give is like a flowing fountain that gives eternal life" (John 4:13-14).

Reflection

Most of us think in a linear fashion most of the time. If we were to map our life on a sheet of paper, for example, we would draw a line from left to right. At the far left end of the line we would position the date of our birth, and at the far right end we would indicate the date of our death. The space between those two points would represent a "lifetime." Thinking about our lives in this way allows us to plan for the future, which is always in the process of opening up for us as we approach the day of our death.

At Christmastime, however, we revert to a previous way of thinking; we think in a more circular fashion. Once again, if we were to map our life on a sheet of paper, we would draw a circle and indicate that somehow the events in our lives have a way of repeating themselves. For example, every Christmas we gather in the homes of our parents or grandparents, or we prepare the same food, or we decorate our home in the same way.

The wreath is a symbol of our circular thinking at Christmastime. A plain, unadorned wreath has no top or bottom, beginning or end. Look at the abundance of wreaths we display at Christmastime. We begin with the Advent wreath, that circular symbol of light and eternal life. We place wreaths on our tables and hang them on our doors and in our windows. The circle represents eternity and the eternal God, who has no beginning and no end. According to John's Gospel, Jesus gives us access to God, who offers us eternal life. Notice that this is life without end—neither linear thinking nor circular thinking, but a combination of the two.

Meditation

Besides wreaths, what other signs of eternity do you find in your home at Christmastime? How does each symbol foster an awareness of the eternal life mediated by Jesus?

Prayer

I praise you, Lord, for being my guide. I will always look to you, as you stand beside me and protect me from fear. With all my heart, I will celebrate, and I can safely rest. You have shown me the path to life, and you make me glad by being near to me (Psalm 16:7-9, 11).

Memories

Make a list of the wreaths you use in your home. For each one, indicate where you use it and the year you bought it, made it, or received it as a gift. Add to this list each year as needed.

Xmas

Scripture

This is the good news about Jesus Christ, the Son of God (Mark 1:1).

Reflection

At this time of year we often see an X for the "Christ" of Christmas. Some people take that as an offense when, in reality, it is merely an abbreviation for Christ. In the Greek alphabet, X *(chi)* represents not only the English "ch," but has become a sign for Christ. Thus "Xmas" is an abbreviation for Christmas, literally "Christ's Mass."

If we look carefully at icons of Jesus, we can see the Greek letters "IS" and "XS" on either side of his head, abbreviations for "Jesus Christ." Some icons portray Jesus as a boy sitting on his mother's lap. Not only is he identified with the Greek abbreviations indicated above, but his mother is also named on either side of her head with "MP" and "THU," Greek abbreviations for "Mother of God." Sometimes we place the X over the P to form a sign for Christ. Since the Greek X represents the English "ch" and the Greek P represents the English "r," we end up with the first three letters of the name "Christ."

Sometimes people think that "Christ" is Jesus' last name. It's not. "Christ" is Greek for "anointed," referring to Jesus as God's chosen one, similar to King David, who is chosen by God and anointed with the horn of oil by Samuel. Jesus of Nazareth is God's Anointed One, whose birth signifies a new beginning for creation.

Meditation

What does Christmas mean to you?

Prayer

Our Lord, I will sing of your love forever. Everyone yet to be born will hear me praise your faithfulness. In a vision, you once said to your faithful followers: "David, my servant, is the one I chose to be king, and I will always be there to help and strengthen him. I have chosen David as my first-born son, and he will be the ruler of all kings on earth. My love for him will last, and my agreement with him will never be broken" (Psalm 89:1, 19-21, 27-28).

Memories

Ask each member of your family what Christmas means to him or her, summarize each person's comments, and date your entries. Modify this list each year as needed.

Yule

Scripture

"I baptize you with water so that you will give up your sins. But someone more powerful is going to come, and I am not good enough even to carry his sandals. He will baptize you with the Holy Spirit and with fire" (Matthew 3:11).

Reflection

"Yule" is a Middle English word for the "Feast of the Nativity of Jesus Christ." We often associate the word with "yule log," a large log put on the hearth on Christmas Eve as the foundation of the fire for Christmas Day. As the log gives off light and warmth, so too is Jesus' birth a fire that lights and warms the world. Thus, the word is also used in reference to the entire season: Yuletide.

Christmas actually begins at sunset on December 24 and continues to the Feast of the Baptism of the Lord, celebrated on the Sunday after the Epiphany or, in some years, on the Monday after the Epiphany. There used to be an emphasis on the "twelve days of Christmas," from December 25 to January 6, in an effort to maintain the spirit of the season. In our consumer-oriented culture, however, this tradition has become difficult to maintain.

The spirit of Christmas is like that of the fire of the Spirit preached by John the Baptist. Keeping the Christmas spirit can be accomplished by leaving decorations in place for the duration of the season. Leave the wreaths on the front door and in the windows, the cards displayed, the candles on the tables. Continue to serve the special foods associated with Christmas. Then, as Yuletide begins to dwindle, ease into Ordinary Time and cherish the spirit of Christmas, which disrupts the routines of our lives.

Meditation

What challenges do you face in trying to keep the spirit of Yuletide present? How can you meet each challenge?

Prayer

You are my God. Show me what you want me to do, and let your gentle Spirit lead me in the right path. Be true to your name, Lord, and keep my life safe (Psalm 143:10-11).

Memories

Make a list of the ways you've managed to keep the Yuletide spirit in years past. Be sure to date your entries. Note how you can keep the Yuletide spirit this year. Add to this list each year as needed.

Zenith

Scripture

"Everyone who has done right will shine like the sun in their Father's kingdom. If you have ears, pay attention!" (Matthew 13:43).

Reflection

The zenith is that point in the sky that is directly overhead. The word often is used metaphorically to refer to a high point of one's life, such as graduating from college, getting an important promotion, or taking a long-dreamed-of trip.

For every person and family, there is a zenith in the midst of each Christmastime. There is something that makes this Christmas special. It might be a tradition or custom, a family activity, or the unique coming together of certain people. The zenith is that one moment, that one event, that gives the most pleasure, becomes memorable, and makes that Christmas unique.

When we reach the end of a Christmas season, reflecting on its high point helps us ease back into our daily routines. It also adds continuity to our lives. The real gift of this holiday season takes it place in our hearts along with all the other cherished memories of holidays past.

Meditation

What has been the zenith of your life to date? What do you continue to long for that might well become the zenith of your entire life?

Prayer

Let the name of the Lord be praised now and forever. From dawn until sunset the name of the Lord deserves to be praised. The Lord is far above all of the nations; he is more glorious than the heavens (Psalm 113:2-4).

Memories

Make a list of the zeniths of the past several Christmases. Date your entries. Do the same in years to come.

Blessings for Advent and Christmastime

Blessing of the Advent Wreath

(*To be used on Saturday evening before the First Sunday of Advent. Usually three of the candles are the same color, and one candle is a different color. No candles are lit for this blessing.*)

Leader: Blessed are you, Lord our God, creator of darkness and light. As the days of winter bring us more hours of darkness, let the light of your Son's birth fill us with the hope of everlasting life. May this wreath remind us of the everlasting crown of glory awaiting us where Jesus is Lord for ever and ever.

All: Amen.

First Week of Advent

(*To be used on the First Sunday of Advent. One of the three candles that are the same color is lit.*)

Leader: May this light shine for ever in our hearts and minds.

All: Amen.

Second Week of Advent

(*To be used on the Saturday before the Second Sunday of Advent. Two of the three candles that are the same color are lit.*)

Leader: Like the light of this wreath, may God shine through the good works of our lives.

All: Amen.

Third Week of Advent

(*To be used on the Saturday before the Third Sunday of Advent. Two of the candles that are the same color are lit, as well as the single candle of a different color.*)

Leader: May God wrap us in the light of grace and prepare us for the birth of Jesus Christ.

All: Amen.

Fourth Week of Advent

(*To be used on the Saturday before the Fourth Sunday of Advent. All four candles are lit.*)

Leader: May the brightness of the risen Lord scatter all the darkness of our lives and make our hearts glow with pure light.

All: Amen.

Blessing of the Tree

Leader: Blessed are you, Lord our God, creator of all trees. Let this tree be a feast for our eyes, and may the gifts under its branches remind us of your gift of Jesus Christ to the world. May this tree and all the trees in the forest shout joyful praise now and forever.

All: Amen.

Blessing of a Creche or Nativity Scene

Leader: Blessed are you, Lord our God, creator of all people. Let this scene remind us of the birth of your Son, Jesus, the crown of the human race. May his humanity remind us of the dignity you have bestowed upon us. Glory to you in the highest now and forever.

All: Amen.

Blessing of the Family

Leader: Blessed are you, Lord our God, creator of all families. Bless and preserve the uniqueness of each person here. Go before us on our pilgrimage and show us the way to you. May we know your presence each day of our lives now and forever.

All: Amen.

Blessing of the Home

Leader: Blessed are you, Lord our God, creator of the earth and its shelters. Come and live in our home and our hearts. May your presence shine in welcome to all those who visit us. May we give you praise now and forever.

All: Amen.

Blessing of Water

(*All gather around a small bowl of water.*)

Leader: Blessed are you, Lord our God, creator of the earth and its oceans, seas, rivers and springs. May this water remind us of your grace, which flows through baptism to us. May this water help us to be grateful to you, the source of all life. All praise be to you for ever and ever. **All:** Amen.

Blessing of Food

Leader: Blessed are you, Lord our God, creator of the earth and all it produces. May this food sustain our bodies, even as your grace sustains our lives. Let this food become a sign of our thanks for this Advent and Christmastime and the many blessings they give to us. May our sharing give you praise for ever and ever.

All: Amen.

Also for the Christmas Season

Winter Skies
A Celtic Christmas
Ian Callanan
A unique collection of sixteen songs, both original compositions and new arrangements of classic Christmas carols, performed by Irish artist Ian Callanan and professional Irish singers and musicians. Performed in a Celtic style that is at once traditional and contemporary. (60-minute compact disc, $14.95)

O Holy Child
The Shepherd's Song
Christmas Carols for Contemporary Christians
Glorious productions of traditional and contemporary Christmas carols on two separate albums, performed by full orchestra and choir. Each album includes two new original Christmas songs and 10-12 traditional carols done in new, upbeat arrangements. (35- to 40-minutes each, compact discs $14.95; audio cassettes, $9.95)

Also by Mark Boyer

Home Is Holy Place
Reflections, Prayers and Meditations
Inspired by the Ordinary
Over thirty reflections on how common household items can enable people to experience the presence of God in their homes. (88 page paperback, $8.95)

A Month-by-Month Guide to Entertaining Angels
Reflections on thirty-six amazing encounters with angels recorded in the Bible, three for each month of the year. (176 page paperback, $11.95)

Available from booksellers or call
800-397-2282 in the U. S. or Canada